CHAIN

To work a chain stitch, begin with a slip knot on the hook. Bring the yarn **over** hook from back to front, catching the yarn with the hook and turning the hook slightly toward you to keep the yarn from slipping off. Draw the yarn through the slip knot *(Fig. 5)* **(first chain stitch made, abbreviated ch)**.

Fig. 5

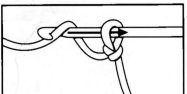

WORKING INTO THE CHAIN

Method 1: Insert hook into back ridge of each chain *(Fig. 6a)*.

Method 2: Insert hook under top two strands of each chain *(Fig. 6b)*.

Fig. 6a

Fig. 6b

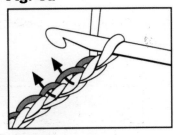 

SLIP STITCH

To work a slip stitch, insert hook in stitch indicated, YO and draw through stitch and through loop on hook *(Fig. 7)* **(slip stitch made, abbreviated slip st)**.

Fig. 7

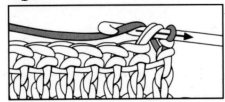

SINGLE

Insert hook in
and draw throu
crochet mad

Fig. 8

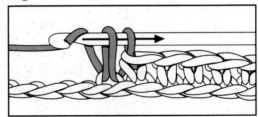

HALF DOUBLE CROCHET

YO, insert hook in stitch indicated, YO and pull up a loop, YO and draw through all 3 loops on hook *(Fig. 9)* **(half double crochet made, abbreviated hdc)**.

Fig. 9

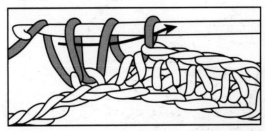

DOUBLE CROCHET

YO, insert hook in stitch indicated, YO and pull up a loop, YO and draw through 2 loops on hook *(Fig. 10a)*, YO and draw through remaining 2 loops on hook *(Fig. 10b)* **(double crochet made, abbreviated dc)**.

Fig. 10a

Fig. 10b

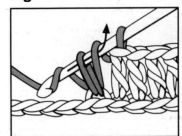 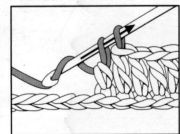

ALUMINUM CROCHET HOOKS												
U.S.	B-1	C-2	D-3	E-4	F-5	G-6	H-8	I-9	J-10	K-10½	N	P	Q
Metric - mm	2.25	2.75	3.25	3.50	3.75	4.00	5.00	5.50	6.00	6.50	9.00	10.00	15.00

1. PARALLEL POSTS

Finished Size: 11" x 11"

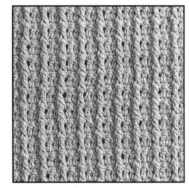

MATERIALS
100% Cotton
Worsted Weight Yarn:
3½ ounces,
(100 grams,
170 yards)
Crochet hook,
size G (4.00 mm)

GAUGE: In pattern,
16 sts and 12 rows = 4"

Ch 42.

Row 1: Dc in fourth ch from hook and in next ch **(3 skipped chs count as first dc)**, ch 1, ★ skip next ch, dc in next 2 chs, ch 1; repeat from ★ across to last 4 chs, skip next ch, dc in last 3 chs: 28 dc and 12 ch-1 sps.

To work **treble crochet (abbreviated tr)**, YO twice, insert hook in st indicated, YO and pull up a loop (4 loops on hook), (YO and draw through 2 loops on hook) 3 times.

Row 2 (Right side): Ch 1, turn; sc in first 3 dc, working in **front** of next ch-1, tr in skipped ch on beginning ch, ★ sc in next 2 dc, working in **front** of next ch-1, tr in skipped ch on beginning ch; repeat from ★ across to last 3 dc, sc in last 3 dc: 28 sc and 12 tr.

Row 3: Ch 3 **(counts as first dc, now and throughout)**, turn; dc in next 2 sc, ch 1, ★ skip next tr, dc in next 2 sc, ch 1; repeat from ★ across to last 4 sts, skip next tr, dc in last 3 sc: 28 dc and 12 ch-1 sps.

To work **Front Post treble crochet (abbreviated FPtr)**, YO twice, insert hook from **front** to **back** around post of next tr one row **below** ch-1 **(Fig. 1, page 1)**, YO and pull up a loop, (YO and draw through 2 loops on hook) 3 times **(counts as one tr)**.

Row 4: Ch 1, turn; sc in first 3 dc, working in **front** of next ch-1, work FPtr, ★ sc in next 2 dc, working in **front** of next ch-1, work FPtr; repeat from ★ across to last 3 dc, sc in last 3 dc: 28 sc and 12 tr.

Row 5: Ch 3, turn; dc in next 2 sc, ch 1, ★ skip next FPtr, dc in next 2 sc, ch 1; repeat from ★ across to last 4 sts, skip next FPtr, dc in last 3 sc: 28 dc and 12 ch-1 sps.

Rows 6-30: Repeat Rows 4 and 5, 12 times; then repeat Row 4 once **more**; do **not** finish off.

EDGING

Rnd 1: Do **not** turn; (ch 3, sc) evenly around, ch 1, hdc in sc at base of beginning ch-3 to form last ch-3 sp.

Rnd 2: Ch 1, sc in same sp, ch 3, dc in third ch from hook, ★ sc in next ch-3 sp, ch 3, dc in third ch from hook; repeat from ★ around; join with slip st to first sc, finish off.

2. RIDGED ROWS

Finished Size: 8" x 9"

MATERIALS
100% Cotton
Worsted Weight Yarn:
1¾ ounces,
(50 grams,
85 yards)
Crochet hook,
size I (5.50 mm)

GAUGE: In pattern,
(sc, ch 1) 10 times and 14 rows = 4"

Ch 40.

Row 1 (Right side): Working in back ridge of ch **(Fig. 4, page 1)**, sc in second ch from hook, ★ ch 1, skip next ch, sc in next ch; repeat from ★ across: 20 sc.

Rows 2-28: Ch 1, turn; working in Back Loops Only **(Fig. 3, page 1)**, sc in first sc, (ch 1, sc in next sc) across; do **not** finish off.

EDGING

Rnd 1: Ch 1, turn; working in Back Loops Only, sc in first sc, ch 1, (sc in next sc, ch 1) across; (sc, ch 1) evenly across end of rows; working in Back Loops Only of beginning ch, sc in first ch, ch 1, ★ skip next ch, sc in next ch, ch 1; repeat from ★ across; (sc, ch 1) evenly across end of rows; join with slip st to first sc.

Rnd 2: Ch 1, do **not** turn; sc in same st, ch 1, (sc in next sc, ch 1) around; join with slip st to first sc, finish off.

3. TREBLE CROSSES _____

Finished Size: 9¼" x 10"

MATERIALS
100% Cotton
  Worsted Weight Yarn:
    2½ ounces,
      (70 grams,
        120 yards)
Crochet hook,
  size G (4.00 mm)

GAUGE: In pattern, (tr, ch 1, tr) 6 times = 4¼";
        4 rows = 2¼"

Ch 39.

Row 1 (Right side): Sc in second ch from hook and in each ch across: 38 sc.

To work **treble crochet (abbreviated tr)**, YO twice, insert hook in st or sp indicated, YO and pull up a loop (4 loops on hook), (YO and draw through 2 loops on hook) 3 times.

Row 2: Ch 3 **(counts as first dc, now and throughout)**, turn; ★ skip next 2 sc, tr in next sc, ch 1, working in **front** of tr just made, tr in first skipped sc **(Cross St made)**; repeat from ★ across to last sc, dc in last sc: 24 tr and 2 dc.

To work **Cluster (uses one ch-1 sp)**, ★ YO, insert hook in ch-1 sp indicated, YO and pull up a loop, YO and draw through 2 loops on hook, YO and draw through one loop on hook; repeat from ★ once **more**, YO and draw through all 3 loops on hook.

Row 3: Ch 5 **(counts as first tr plus ch 1)**, turn; work Cluster in next ch-1 sp, (ch 2, work Cluster in next ch-1 sp) across to last 2 sts, ch 1, skip next tr, tr in last dc: 12 Clusters and 13 sps.

Row 4: Ch 3, turn; skip first ch-1 sp, tr in next ch-2 sp, ch 1, working **behind** tr just made, tr in skipped ch-1 sp **(Cross St made)**, ★ tr in next sp, ch 1, working **behind** tr just made, tr in same sp as first tr of last Cross St; repeat from ★ across to last tr, dc in last tr: 12 Cross Sts.

Row 5: Ch 1, turn; sc in each st and in each ch-1 sp across: 38 sc.

Rows 6-17: Repeat Rows 2-5, 3 times; do **not** finish off.

EDGING
Ch 3, do **not** turn; dc evenly around entire piece working (2 dc, ch 2, 2 dc) in each corner; join with slip st to first dc, finish off.

4. LOADED V-STS _____

Finished Size: 10" x 9¼"

MATERIALS
100% Cotton
  Worsted Weight Yarn:
    2½ ounces,
      (70 grams,
        120 yards)
Crochet hook,
  size H (5.00 mm)

GAUGE: In pattern,
        15 sts = 4"; 12 rows = 4¼"

Ch 34.

Row 1: Sc in second ch from hook and in each ch across: 33 sc.

Row 2 (Right side): Ch 3 **(counts as first dc, now and throughout)**, turn; ★ skip next sc, (dc, ch 1, dc) in next sc, skip next sc, dc in next sc; repeat from ★ across: 25 dc and 8 ch-1 sps.

Row 3: Ch 1, turn; sc in first dc, ★ ch 3, skip next 2 dc, sc in next dc; repeat from ★ across: 9 sc and 8 ch-3 sps.

To work **Long Single Crochet (abbreviated LSC)**, working around ch-3, insert hook in ch-1 sp indicated, YO and pull up a loop even with last st made, YO and draw through both loops on hook **(counts as one sc)**.

Row 4: Ch 1, turn; sc in first sc, ★ work 3 LSC in next ch-1 sp **below** ch-3, sc in next sc; repeat from ★ across.

Rows 5-23: Repeat Rows 2-4, 6 times; then repeat Row 2 once **more**.

Row 24: Ch 1, turn; sc in each dc and in each ch-1 sp across; do **not** finish off: 33 sc.

EDGING
Rnd 1: Ch 1, do **not** turn; sc evenly around entire piece working a number of sc that is divisible by 3 and working 3 sc in each corner; join with slip st to first sc.

To **decrease**, pull up a loop in next 2 sc, YO and draw through all 3 loops on hook.

Rnd 2: Ch 1, sc in same st, ch 1, decrease, ch 1, ★ sc in next sc, ch 1, decrease, ch 1; repeat from ★ around; join with slip st to first sc, finish off.

5. CHAINED COLUMNS

Finished Size: 9½" x 9"

MATERIALS
100% Cotton
  Worsted Weight Yarn:
    1¾ ounces,
      (50 grams,
        85 yards)
  Crochet hook,
    size I (5.50 mm)

GAUGE: In pattern,
    2 sc, (ch 2, 2 sc) 3 times and 13 rows = 3½"

Ch 35.

Row 1 (Right side): Sc in second ch from hook and in next ch, ★ ch 2, skip next 2 chs, sc in next 2 chs; repeat from ★ across: 18 sc.

Rows 2-32: Ch 1, turn; sc in first 2 sc, (ch 2, sc in next 2 sc) across; do **not** finish off.

EDGING
Rnd 1: Ch 1, turn; sc evenly around entire piece working an even number of sc and working 3 sc in each corner; join with slip st to first sc.

Rnd 2: Ch 1, do **not** turn; sc in same st, slip st in next sc, (sc in next sc, slip st in next sc) around; join with slip st to first sc, finish off.

6. SLANT SHELLS

Finished Size: 10" x 10"

MATERIALS
100% Cotton
  Worsted Weight Yarn:
    3 ounces,
      (90 grams,
        145 yards)
  Crochet hook,
    size F (3.50 mm)

GAUGE: In pattern, 12 sts and 8 rows = 3¼"

Ch 32.

Row 1: Sc in second ch from hook, ★ ch 1, skip next ch, sc in next ch; repeat from ★ across: 16 sc and 15 ch-1 sps.

Row 2 (Right side): Ch 3 **(counts as first dc, now and throughout)**, turn; dc in same st, ch 1, slip st in next ch-1 sp, ch 1, ★ skip next sc, 3 dc in next ch-1 sp, ch 1, skip next sc, slip st in next ch-1 sp, ch 1; repeat from ★ across to last sc, 2 dc in last sc: 25 dc.

Row 3: Ch 1, turn; sc in first dc, ★ skip next ch-1 sp, dc in next ch-1 sp, ch 2, skip next dc, sc in next dc; repeat from ★ across: 17 sts and 8 ch-2 sps.

Row 4: Ch 3, turn; dc in same st, ch 1, slip st in next ch-2 sp, ch 1, ★ 3 dc in next sc, ch 1, slip st in next ch-2 sp, ch 1; repeat from ★ across to last 2 sts, skip next dc, 2 dc in last sc: 25 dc.

Row 5: Ch 1, turn; sc in first dc, ★ ch 2, dc in next ch-1 sp, skip next dc, sc in next dc; repeat from ★ across: 17 sts and 8 ch-2 sps.

Row 6: Ch 3, turn; dc in same st, ch 1, slip st in next ch-2 sp, ch 1, ★ 3 dc in next sc, ch 1, slip st in next ch-2 sp, ch 1; repeat from ★ across to last sc, 2 dc in last sc: 25 dc.

Rows 7-23: Repeat Rows 3-6, 4 times; then repeat Row 3 once **more**.

Row 24: Ch 1, turn; sc in first sc, ★ ch 1, sc in next ch-2 sp, ch 1, skip next dc, sc in next sc; repeat from ★ across; do **not** finish off: 17 sc and 16 ch-1 sps.

EDGING
Rnd 1: Ch 1, do **not** turn; sc evenly around entire piece working a number of sc that is divisible by 3 and working 3 sc in each corner; join with slip st to first sc.

To **decrease**, pull up a loop in next 2 sc, YO and draw through all 3 loops on hook.

Rnd 2: Ch 1, sc in same st, ch 1, decrease, ch 1, ★ sc in next sc, ch 1, decrease, ch 1; repeat from ★ around; join with slip st to first sc, finish off.

7. SINGLE CROSSES

Finished Size: 9½" x 10"

MATERIALS
 100% Cotton
  Worsted Weight Yarn:
   2¼ ounces,
    (65 grams,
     110 yards)
 Crochet hook,
  size I (5.50 mm)

GAUGE: In pattern, 18 sts and 13 rows = 4"

Ch 39.

Row 1 (Wrong side)**:** Sc in second ch from hook, ★ skip next ch, sc in next ch, working **loosely** around sc just made, sc in skipped ch; repeat from ★ across to last ch, sc in last ch: 38 sc.

Rows 2-28: Ch 1, turn; sc in first sc, ★ skip next sc, sc in next sc, working **loosely** around sc just made, sc in skipped sc; repeat from ★ across to last sc, sc in last sc; do **not** finish off.

EDGING
Rnd 1: Ch 1, do **not** turn; sc evenly around entire piece working an even number of sc and working 3 sc in each corner; join with slip st to first sc.

Rnd 2: Ch 1, sc in each sc around working 2 sc in center sc of each corner; join with slip st to first sc.

Rnd 3: Ch 1, sc in next sc, working **loosely** around sc just made, sc in same st as joining, ★ skip next sc, sc in next sc, working **loosely** around sc just made, sc in skipped sc; repeat from ★ around; join with slip st to first sc, finish off.

8. DC TRAILS

Finished Size: 10" x 8¾"

MATERIALS
 100% Cotton
  Worsted Weight Yarn:
   2¼ ounces,
    (65 grams,
     110 yards)
 Crochet hook,
  size I (5.50 mm)

GAUGE: In pattern,
  17 sts = 4"; 16 rows = 4¼"

Ch 40.

Row 1: Sc in second ch from hook and in each ch across: 39 sc.

Row 2 (Right side)**:** Ch 1, turn; sc in first sc, ★ ch 1, skip next sc, sc in next sc; repeat from ★ across: 20 sc and 19 ch-1 sps.

Row 3: Ch 1, turn; sc in first sc and in next ch-1 sp, (ch 1, sc in next ch-1 sp) across to last sc, sc in last sc: 21 sc and 18 ch-1 sps.

Row 4: Ch 1, turn; sc in first sc, ch 1, (sc in next ch-1 sp, ch 1) across to last 2 sc, skip next sc, sc in last sc: 20 sc and 19 ch-1 sps.

Rows 5 and 6: Repeat Rows 3 and 4.

Row 7: Ch 1, turn; sc in each sc and in each ch-1 sp across: 39 sc.

Row 8: Ch 3 **(counts as first dc)**, turn; dc in Back Loop Only of next sc **(Fig. 3, page 1)**, dc in Front Loop Only of next sc, ★ dc in **both** loops of next sc, dc in Back Loop Only of next sc, dc in Front Loop Only of next sc; repeat from ★ across.

Row 9: Ch 1, turn; sc in Front Loop Only of first dc, ★ sc in Back Loop Only of next dc, sc in Front Loop Only of next dc; repeat from ★ across.

Row 10: Ch 1, turn; working in both loops, sc in first sc, ★ ch 1, skip next sc, sc in next sc; repeat from ★ across: 20 sc and 19 ch-1 sps.

Rows 11-31: Repeat Rows 3-10 twice, then repeat Rows 3-7 once **more**; do **not** finish off.

EDGING
Rnd 1: Ch 1, turn; sc evenly around entire piece working 3 sc in each corner; join with slip st to first sc.

Rnd 2: Do **not** turn; slip st **loosely** in each sc around; join with slip st to joining slip st, finish off.

9. CLIMBING V-STS

Finished Size:
9½" x 8¾"

MATERIALS
100% Cotton
Worsted Weight Yarn:
2¼ ounces,
(65 grams,
110 yards)
Crochet hook,
size I (5.50 mm)

GAUGE: In pattern, 11 sts = 3";
13 rows = 3½"

Ch 32.

Row 1 (Right side)**:** Sc in second ch from hook and in each ch across: 31 sc.

Row 2: Ch 1, turn; sc in each sc across.

To work **V-St,** (dc, ch 2, dc) in next sc.

Row 3: Ch 1, turn; sc in first 2 sc, skip next sc, work V-St, skip next sc, sc in next sc, skip next sc, work V-St, skip next sc, ★ sc in next 3 sc, skip next sc, work V-St, skip next sc, sc in next sc, skip next sc, work V-St, skip next sc; repeat from ★ once **more**, sc in last 2 sc: 25 sts and 6 ch-2 sps.

Row 4: Ch 1, turn; sc in first 2 sc, ch 3, skip next V-St, sc in next sc, ch 3, skip next V-St, ★ sc in next 3 sc, ch 3, skip next V-St, sc in next sc, ch 3, skip next V-St; repeat from ★ once **more**, sc in last 2 sc: 13 sc and 6 ch-3 sps.

To work **Long Single Crochet** *(abbreviated LSC),* working around ch-3, insert hook in ch-2 sp indicated, YO and pull up a loop even with last st made, YO and draw through both loops on hook **(counts as one sc)**.

Row 5: Ch 1, turn; sc in first 2 sc and in next ch-3 sp, ★ † work LSC in ch-2 sp **below** ch-3, sc in same ch-3 sp and in next sc, sc in next ch-3 sp, work LSC in ch-2 sp **below** ch-3, sc in same ch-3 sp †, sc in next 3 sc and in next ch-3 sp; repeat from ★ once **more**, then repeat from † to † once, sc in last 2 sc: 31 sc.

Rows 6-29: Repeat Rows 2-5, 6 times; do **not** finish off.

EDGING

Rnd 1: Ch 1, do **not** turn; sc evenly around entire piece working a number of sc that is divisible by 3 and working 3 sc in each corner; join with slip st to first sc.

To **decrease**, pull up a loop in next 2 sc, YO and draw through all 3 loops on hook.

Rnd 2: Ch 1, sc in same st, ch 1, decrease, ch 1, ★ sc in next sc, ch 1, decrease, ch 1; repeat from ★ around; join with slip st to first sc, finish off.

10. SINGLE COLUMNS

Finished Size: 8½" x 9"

MATERIALS
100% Cotton
Worsted Weight Yarn:
1¾ ounces,
(50 grams,
85 yards)
Crochet hook,
size I (5.50 mm)

GAUGE: In pattern,
15 sts and 10 rows = 3"

Ch 41.

Row 1 (Right side)**:** Sc in second ch from hook, (ch 1, skip next ch, sc in next ch) twice, ★ ch 2, skip next 2 chs, sc in next ch, (ch 1, skip next ch, sc in next ch) twice; repeat from ★ across: 18 sc and 17 sps.

Rows 2-28: Ch 1, turn; working in Back Loops Only *(Fig. 3, page 1)*, sc in first sc, (ch 1, sc in next sc) twice, ★ ch 2, sc in next sc, (ch 1, sc in next sc) twice; repeat from ★ across; do **not** finish off.

EDGING

Rnd 1: Ch 1, turn; sc evenly around entire piece working 3 sc in each corner; join with slip st to first sc.

Rnd 2: Do **not** turn; slip st **loosely** in each sc around; join with slip st to joining slip st, finish off.

11. LONGBRANCH SINGLES

Finished Size: 9½" x 10"

MATERIALS
100% Cotton
  Worsted Weight Yarn:
    2¼ ounces,
      (65 grams,
        110 yards)
Crochet hook,
  size G (4.00 mm)

GAUGE: In pattern,
  16 sts and 13 rows = 4"

Ch 36.

Row 1 (Right side): Sc in second ch from hook and in each ch across: 35 sc.

Row 2: Ch 1, turn; sc in first sc, ★ ch 1, skip next sc, sc in next sc; repeat from ★ across: 18 sc and 17 ch-1 sps.

Row 3: Ch 1, turn; sc in first sc and in next ch-1 sp, ★ ch 3, skip next ch-1 sp, sc in next ch-1 sp; repeat from ★ across to last sc, sc in last sc: 11 sc and 8 ch-3 sps.

To work **Long Single Crochet** *(abbreviated LSC)*, working around ch-3, insert hook in ch-1 sp indicated, YO and pull up a loop even with last st made, YO and draw through both loops on hook **(counts as one sc)**.

Row 4: Ch 1, turn; sc in first 2 sc, ch 1, work LSC in next ch-1 sp **below** ch-3, ch 1, ★ sc in next sc, ch 1, work LSC in next ch-1 sp **below** ch-3, ch 1; repeat from ★ across to last 2 sc, sc in last 2 sc: 19 sc and 16 ch-1 sps.

Row 5: Ch 1, turn; sc in first sc, ch 1, skip next sc, (sc in next ch-1 sp, ch 1) across to last 2 sc, skip next sc, sc in last sc: 18 sc and 17 ch-1 sps.

Row 6: Ch 1, turn; sc in each sc and in each ch-1 sp across: 35 sc.

Rows 7-36: Repeat Rows 2-6, 6 times; do **not** finish off.

EDGING
Rnd 1: Ch 1, turn; sc evenly around entire piece working 3 sc in each corner; join with slip st to first sc.

To work **Twisted single crochet** *(abbreviated Twisted sc)*, working **loosely**, insert hook in st indicated, YO and pull up a loop (2 loops on hook), twist loops on hook by rotating hook clockwise once, YO and draw through both loops on hook.

Rnd 2: Ch 1, do **not** turn; work Twisted sc in each sc around; join with slip st to first st, finish off.

12. LATTICE

Finished Size: 9" x 9"

MATERIALS
100% Cotton
  Worsted Weight Yarn:
    1¾ ounces,
      (50 grams,
        85 yards)
Crochet hook,
  size I (5.50 mm)

GAUGE: In pattern,
  12 sts = 4"; 10 rows = 4¼"

Ch 34.

Row 1 (Right side): Sc in second ch from hook, ★ skip next ch, dc in next ch, ch 2, dc around post of dc just made, skip next ch, sc in next ch; repeat from ★ across: 9 sc and 8 ch-2 sps.

Row 2: Ch 4 **(counts as first dc plus ch 1)**, turn; sc in next ch-2 sp, ch 1, skip next dc, dc in next sc, ★ ch 1, sc in next ch-2 sp, ch 1, skip next dc, dc in next sc; repeat from ★ across: 17 sts and 16 ch-1 sps.

Row 3: Ch 1, turn; sc in first dc, ★ skip next ch-1 sp, dc in next sc, ch 2, dc around post of dc just made, skip next ch-1 sp, sc in next dc; repeat from ★ across.

Rows 4-18: Repeat Rows 2 and 3, 7 times; then repeat Row 2 once **more**; do **not** finish off.

EDGING
Rnd 1: Ch 1, turn; sc evenly around entire piece working an even number of sc and working 3 sc in each corner; join with slip st to first sc.

Rnd 2: Ch 1, do **not** turn; sc in next sc, working **loosely** around sc just made, sc in same st as joining, ★ skip next sc, sc in next sc, working **loosely** around sc just made, sc in skipped sc; repeat from ★ around; join with slip st to first sc, finish off.

13. BARGELLO CHAINS _____

Finished Size: 8¾" x 10"

MATERIALS
100% Cotton
Worsted Weight Yarn:
1¾ ounces,
(50 grams,
85 yards)
Crochet hook,
size I (5.50 mm)

GAUGE: In pattern,
sc, (ch 2, sc) 5 times and 13 rows = 4"

Ch 32.

Row 1 (Right side): Sc in second ch from hook, ★ ch 2, skip next 2 chs, sc in next ch; repeat from ★ across: 11 sc and 10 ch-2 sps.

Rows 2-29: Ch 1, turn; sc in first sc, (ch 2, sc in next sc) across; do **not** finish off.

EDGING
Rnd 1: Ch 1, do **not** turn; sc evenly around entire piece working 3 sc in each corner; join with slip st to first sc.

Rnd 2: Ch 1, sc in same st and in each sc around; join with slip st to first sc, finish off.

14. RAILED CLUSTERS _____

Finished Size: 9" x 8½"

MATERIALS
100% Cotton
Worsted Weight Yarn:
2½ ounces,
(70 grams,
120 yards)
Crochet hook,
size J (6.00 mm)

GAUGE: In pattern, 14 dc and Rows 1-9 = 4"

Ch 33.

Row 1 (Right side): Dc in fourth ch from hook **(3 skipped chs count as first dc)** and in each ch across: 31 dc.

Row 2: Ch 1, turn; sc in first dc, ★ ch 1, skip next dc, sc in next dc; repeat from ★ across: 16 sc and 15 ch-1 sps.

To work **Cluster** (uses one ch-1 sp), ★ YO, insert hook in ch-1 sp indicated, YO and pull up a loop, YO and draw through 2 loops on hook, YO and draw through one loop on hook; repeat from ★ 2 times **more**, YO and draw through all 4 loops on hook.

Row 3: Ch 3 **(counts as first dc, now and throughout)**, turn; dc in next ch-1 sp, ★ ch 1, work Cluster in next ch-1 sp, ch 1, dc in next ch-1 sp; repeat from ★ across to last sc, dc in last sc: 7 Clusters and 10 dc.

Row 4: Ch 1, turn; sc in first dc, ch 1, (sc in next ch-1 sp, ch 1) across to last 2 dc, skip next dc, sc in last dc: 16 sc and 15 ch-1 sps.

Row 5: Ch 3, turn; dc in each ch-1 sp and in each sc across: 31 dc.

Rows 6-17: Repeat Rows 2-5, 3 times; do **not** finish off.

EDGING
Rnd 1: Ch 1, do **not** turn; sc evenly around entire piece working a number of sc that is divisible by 3 and working 3 sc in each corner; join with slip st to Back Loop Only of first sc *(Fig. 3, page 1)*.

Rnd 2: Slip st **loosely** in Back Loop Only of each sc around; join with slip st to Back Loop Only of joining slip st.

To **decrease,** pull up a loop in next 2 slip sts, YO and draw through all 3 loops on hook.

Rnd 3: Ch 1, working in Back Loops Only, sc in same st, ch 1, decrease, ch 1, ★ sc in next slip st, ch 1, decrease, ch 1; repeat from ★ around; join with slip st to **both** loops of first sc, finish off.

15. PEEPHOLE SINGLES

Finished Size:
10½" x 10"

MATERIALS
100% Cotton
Worsted Weight Yarn:
2¾ ounces,
(80 grams,
130 yards)
Crochet hook,
size J (6.00 mm)

GAUGE: In pattern, 13 sts and 15 rows = 4"

Ch 34.

Row 1: Sc in second ch from hook, ch 1, skip next ch, sc in next ch, ★ ch 2, skip next 2 chs, sc in next ch, ch 1, skip next ch, sc in next ch; repeat from ★ across: 14 sc and 13 sps.

Row 2 (Right side)**:** Ch 1, turn; sc in first sc, ch 1, sc in next sc, ★ ch 2, sc in next sc, ch 1, sc in next sc; repeat from ★ across.

To work **Long Single Crochet** *(abbreviated LSC),* working around next ch, insert hook in sp indicated, YO and pull up a loop even with last st made, YO and draw through both loops on hook **(counts as one sc)**.

Row 3: Ch 1, turn; sc in first sc, ch 1, sc in next sc, ★ work 2 LSC in next ch-2 sp one row **below** ch-2, sc in next sc, ch 1, sc in next sc; repeat from ★ across.

Row 4: Ch 1, turn; sc in first sc, work LSC in next ch-1 sp one row **below** ch-1, sc in next sc, ★ ch 2, skip next 2 sc, sc in next sc, work LSC in next ch-1 sp one row **below** ch-1, sc in next sc; repeat from ★ across.

Row 5: Ch 1, turn; sc in first sc, ch 1, skip next sc, sc in next sc, ★ ch 2, sc in next sc, ch 1, skip next sc, sc in next sc; repeat from ★ across.

Rows 6-33: Repeat Rows 3-5, 9 times; then repeat Row 3 once **more**.

Row 34: Ch 1, turn; sc in first sc, ch 1, sc in next sc, ★ ch 2, skip next 2 sc, sc in next sc, ch 1, sc in next sc; repeat from ★ across; do **not** finish off: 14 sc and 13 sps.

EDGING
Rnd 1: Ch 1, do **not** turn; sc evenly around entire piece working 3 sc in each corner; join with slip st to first sc.

Rnd 2: Slip st **loosely** in each sc around; join with slip st to first slip st, finish off.

16. UPRAISED V-STS

Finished Size:
8¾" x 9¼"

MATERIALS
100% Cotton
Worsted Weight Yarn:
2 ounces,
(60 grams,
95 yards)
Crochet hook,
size F (3.50 mm)

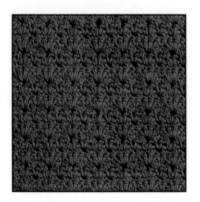

GAUGE: In pattern, 14 sts and 12 rows = 3½"

Ch 32.

Row 1 (Right side)**:** Sc in second ch from hook, ★ ch 1, skip next ch, sc in next ch; repeat from ★ across: 16 sc and 15 ch-1 sps.

Row 2: Ch 1, turn; sc in first sc and in next ch-1 sp, ★ work V-St in next ch-1 sp, sc in next ch-1 sp; repeat from ★ across to last sc, sc in last sc: 10 sc and 7 V-Sts.

Row 3: Ch 1, turn; sc in first 2 sc, ch 3, ★ skip next V-St, sc in next sc, ch 3; repeat from ★ across to last 2 sc, sc in last 2 sc: 10 sc and 7 ch-3 sps.

To work **Long Single Crochet** *(abbreviated LSC),* working around ch-3, insert hook in sp indicated, YO and pull up a loop even with last st made, YO and draw through both loops on hook **(counts as one sc)**.

Row 4: Ch 1, turn; sc in first 2 sc, work 3 LSC in next V-St (ch-1 sp) one row **below** ch-3, ★ sc in next sc, work 3 LSC in next V-St one row **below** ch-3; repeat from ★ across to last 2 sc, sc in last 2 sc: 31 sc.

Row 5: Ch 1, turn; sc in first sc, ★ ch 1, skip next sc, sc in next sc; repeat from ★ across: 16 sc and 15 ch-1 sps.

Rows 6-29: Repeat Rows 2-5, 6 times; do **not** finish off.

EDGING
Rnd 1: Ch 1, do **not** turn; sc evenly around entire piece working a number of sc that is divisible by 3 and working 3 sc in each corner; join with slip st to first sc.

To **decrease**, pull up a loop in next 2 sc, YO and draw through all 3 loops on hook.

Rnd 2: Ch 1, sc in same st, ch 1, decrease, ch 1, ★ sc in next sc, ch 1, decrease, ch 1; repeat from ★ around; join with slip st to first sc, finish off.

17. DOUBLE TREBLE CROSSES

Finished Size: 9½" x 10"

MATERIALS
100% Cotton
  Worsted Weight Yarn:
    2½ ounces,
      (70 grams,
        120 yards)
  Crochet hook,
    size F (3.50 mm)

GAUGE: In pattern,
  12 sts = 3"; 7 rows = 3¼"

Ch 35.

Row 1 (Right side): Sc in second ch from hook and in each ch across: 34 sc.

To work **treble crochet** *(abbreviated tr)*, YO twice, insert hook in sc indicated, YO and pull up a loop (4 loops on hook), (YO and draw through 2 loops on hook) 3 times.

Row 2: Ch 4 **(counts as first tr)**, turn; ★ skip next 2 sc, tr in next 2 sc, working **behind** 2 tr just made, tr in first skipped sc and in next skipped sc; repeat from ★ across to last sc, tr in last sc.

Row 3: Ch 1, turn; sc in each tr across.

Rows 4-19: Repeat Rows 2 and 3, 8 times; do **not** finish off.

EDGING

To work **Puff St**, YO, insert hook in next st or sp, YO and pull up a loop even with loop on hook, ★ YO, insert hook in same st or sp, YO and pull up a loop even with loop on hook; repeat from ★ once **more**, YO and draw through all 7 loops on hook.

Pull up a ½" loop, do **not** turn; work Puff Sts evenly around entire piece working (Puff St, ch 3, Puff St) in each corner; join with slip st to first Puff St, finish off.

18. SOFT CLUSTERS

Finished Size: 9" x 9½"

MATERIALS
100% Cotton
  Worsted Weight Yarn:
    1¾ ounces,
      (50 grams,
        85 yards)
  Crochet hook,
    size F (3.50 mm)

GAUGE: In pattern,
  (sc, ch 1) 8 times = 4¼"; 11 rows = 4"

Ch 32.

Row 1: Sc in second ch from hook, ★ ch 1, skip next ch, sc in next ch; repeat from ★ across: 16 sc and 15 ch-1 sps.

Row 2 (Right side)**:** Ch 1, turn; sc in first sc, (ch 1, sc in next sc) across.

Row 3: Ch 1, turn; sc in first sc, (ch 1, sc in next sc) across.

To work **Cluster** (uses one ch-1 sp), ★ YO, insert hook in sp indicated, YO and pull up a loop, YO and draw through 2 loops on hook; repeat from ★ once **more**, YO and draw through all 3 loops on hook.

Row 4: Ch 4 **(counts as first dc plus ch 1)**, turn; (work Cluster in next ch-1 sp, ch 1) across to last sc, dc in last sc: 15 Clusters.

Row 5: Ch 1, turn; sc in first dc, ch 1, skip next ch-1 sp, (sc in next ch-1 sp, ch 1) across to last ch-1 sp, skip last ch-1 sp, sc in last dc: 16 sc and 15 ch-1 sps.

Rows 6 and 7: Ch 1, turn; sc in first sc, (ch 1, sc in next sc) across.

Rows 8-23: Repeat Rows 4-7, 4 times; do **not** finish off.

EDGING
Rnd 1: Ch 1, turn; sc evenly around entire piece working an even number of sc and working 3 sc in each corner; join with slip st to first sc.

Rnd 2: Ch 1, do **not** turn; sc in next sc, working **loosely** around sc just made, sc in same st as joining, ★ skip next sc, sc in next sc, working **loosely** around sc just made, sc in skipped sc; repeat from ★ around; join with slip st to first sc, finish off.

19. DOUBLE CROSSES

Finished Size:
10¾" x 10¾"

MATERIALS
100% Cotton
  Worsted Weight Yarn:
    2¾ ounces,
      (80 grams,
        130 yards)
  Crochet hook,
    size F (3.50 mm)

GAUGE: In pattern, 16 dc and 8 rows = 4"

Ch 38.

Row 1 (Wrong side)**:** Dc in fourth ch from hook
(3 skipped chs count as first dc), ★ skip next ch, dc
in next ch, working **behind** dc just made, dc in skipped
ch; repeat from ★ across to last 2 chs, dc in last 2 chs:
36 dc.

Rows 2-18: Ch 3 **(counts as first dc)**, turn; dc in
next dc, ★ skip next dc, dc in next dc, working **behind** dc
just made, dc in skipped dc; repeat from ★ across to last
2 dc, dc in last 2 dc; do **not** finish off.

EDGING
Rnd 1: Ch 1, do **not** turn; 2 sc in same st, work 35 sc
evenly spaced across to next corner, ★ 3 sc in corner,
work 35 sc evenly spaced across to next corner; repeat
from ★ 2 times **more**, sc in same st as first sc; join with
slip st to first sc: 152 sc.

Rnd 2: Ch 4, (dc in same st, ch 1) twice, ★ skip next sc,
(dc in next sc, ch 1, skip next sc) across to center sc of
next corner 3-sc group, (dc, ch 1) 3 times in center sc;
repeat from ★ 2 times **more**, skip next sc, (dc in next sc,
ch 1, skip next sc) across; join with slip st to third ch of
beginning ch-4: 84 ch-1 sps.

To work **treble crochet (abbreviated tr)**, YO twice,
working in **front** of sp indicated, insert hook in st
indicated, YO and pull up a loop (4 loops on hook), (YO
and draw through 2 loops on hook) 3 times.

Rnd 3: Ch 1, sc in same st, tr in corner sc on Rnd 1
below next ch-1, sc in next dc, tr in same st on Rnd 1 as
last tr, sc in next dc, ★ (tr in skipped sc on Rnd 1 **below**
next ch-1, sc in next dc) 19 times, tr in corner sc on
Rnd 1 **below** next ch-1, sc in next dc, tr in same st on
Rnd 1 as last tr, sc in next dc; repeat from ★ 2 times
more, tr in skipped sc on Rnd 1 **below** next ch-1, (sc in
next dc, tr in skipped sc on Rnd 1 **below** next ch-1)
across; join with slip st to first sc, finish off.

20. POSTED V-STS

Finished Size: 10" x 9"

MATERIALS
100% Cotton
  Worsted Weight Yarn:
    2¾ ounces,
      (80 grams,
        130 yards)
  Crochet hook,
    size G (4.00 mm)

GAUGE: In pattern,
      14 dc = 4"; 8 rows = 3¾"

Ch 41.

Row 1 (Right side)**:** Dc in fourth ch from hook
(3 skipped chs count as first dc), skip next ch, (dc,
ch 1, dc) in next ch, ★ skip next ch, dc in next ch, skip
next ch, (dc, ch 1, dc) in next ch; repeat from ★ across to
last 3 chs, skip next ch, dc in last 2 chs: 30 dc and
9 ch-1 sps.

To work **Front Post double crochet (abbreviated
FPdc)**, YO, insert hook from **front** to **back** around post
of st indicated **(Fig. 1, page 1)**, YO and pull up a loop (3
loops on hook), (YO and draw through 2 loops on hook)
twice.

Row 2: Ch 3 **(counts as first dc, now and
throughout)**, work FPdc around next dc, ★ (dc, ch 1, dc)
in next ch-1 sp, skip next dc, work FPdc around next dc;
repeat from ★ across to last dc, dc in last dc.

Rows 3-16: Ch 3, turn; work FPdc around next FPdc,
★ (dc, ch 1, dc) in next ch-1 sp, skip next dc, work FPdc
around next FPdc; repeat from ★ across to last dc, dc in
last dc; do **not** finish off.

EDGING
Rnd 1: Ch 1, turn; 2 sc in same st, sc in each dc and in
each ch-1 sp across to last dc, 3 sc in last dc; work 35 sc
evenly spaced across end of rows; working in free loops
of beginning ch **(Fig. 2b, page 1)**, 3 sc in first ch, sc in
next 37 chs, 3 sc in next ch; work 35 sc evenly spaced
across end of rows, sc in same st as first sc; join with
slip st to Back Loop Only of first sc **(Fig. 3, page 1)**: 156 sc.

Rnd 2: Ch 3, do **not** turn; 2 dc in Back Loop Only of
same st, ★ dc in Back Loop Only of next sc, (dc in Front
Loop Only of next sc, dc in Back Loop Only of next sc)
across to center sc of next corner 3-sc group, 3 dc in
Back Loop Only of center sc; repeat from ★ 2 times
more, dc in Back Loop Only of next sc, (dc in Front
Loop Only of next sc, dc in Back Loop Only of next sc)
across; join with slip st to first dc, finish off.

21. DUAL CLUSTERS

Finished Size: 10" x 9¼"

MATERIALS
100% Cotton
Worsted Weight Yarn:
2¼ ounces,
(65 grams,
110 yards)
Crochet hook,
size I (5.50 mm)

GAUGE: In pattern,
11 sts and 9 rows = 3"

FIRST SIDE
Ch 32.

Row 1: Sc in back ridge of second ch from hook and each ch across *(Fig. 4, page 1)*: 31 sc.

Row 2 (Right side)**:** Ch 1, turn; sc in first sc, ★ ch 1, skip next sc, sc in next sc; repeat from ★ across: 16 sc and 15 ch-1 sps.

Note: Loop a short piece of yarn around any stitch to mark Row 2 as **right** side.

Row 3: Ch 3 **(counts as first dc)**, turn; dc in same st, ch 1, slip st in next ch-1 sp, ch 1, ★ 3 dc in next ch-1 sp, ch 1, slip st in next ch-1 sp, ch 1; repeat from ★ across to last sc, 2 dc in last sc: 25 dc and 16 ch-1 sps.

To **decrease** (uses next 2 ch-1 sps), ★ YO, insert hook in **next** ch-1 sp, YO and pull up a loop, YO and draw through 2 loops on hook; repeat from ★ once **more**, YO and draw through all 3 loops on hook **(counts as one dc)**.

Row 4: Ch 1, turn; sc in first dc, decrease, ★ ch 1, skip next dc, sc in next dc, ch 1, decrease; repeat from ★ across to last 2 dc, skip next dc, sc in next dc: 17 sts and 14 ch-1 sps.

Row 5: Ch 1, turn; sc in each st and in each ch-1 sp across: 31 sc.

Row 6: Ch 1, turn; sc in first sc, ★ ch 1, skip next sc, sc in next sc; repeat from ★ across: 16 sc and 15 ch-1 sps.

Rows 7-13: Repeat Rows 3-6 once, then repeat Rows 3-5 once **more**.

Finish off.

SECOND SIDE
Row 1: With **right** side facing and working in free loops of beginning ch *(Fig. 2b, page 1)*, join yarn with sc in first ch *(see Joining With Sc, page 1)*; ★ ch 1, skip next ch, sc in next ch; repeat from ★ across: 16 sc and 15 ch-1 sps.

Rows 2-12: Work same as Rows 3-13 of First Side; do **not** finish off.

EDGING
Rnd 1: Ch 1, turn; sc in each sc across to last sc, (sc, ch 1, sc) in last sc; † working in end of rows, skip first row, sc in next 2 rows, dc in next 3 rows, (sc in next row, dc in next 3 rows) 4 times, sc in next 2 rows, skip last row †; working across last row of First Side, (sc, ch 1, sc) in first sc, sc in each sc across to last sc, (sc, ch 1, sc) in last sc; repeat from † to † once, sc in same st as first sc, ch 1; join with slip st to first sc: 112 sts and 4 ch-1 sps.

To work **Twisted single crochet (abbreviated Twisted sc)**, working **loosely**, insert hook in st indicated, YO and pull up a loop (2 loops on hook), twist loops on hook by rotating hook clockwise once, YO and draw through both loops on hook.

Rnd 2: Ch 1, do **not** turn; ★ work Twisted sc in each st across to next corner ch-1 sp, work 2 Twisted sc in corner ch-1 sp; repeat from ★ around; join with slip st to first st, finish off.

22. TRELLIS POSTS

Finished Size:
10" x 10½"

MATERIALS
100% Cotton
  Worsted Weight Yarn:
    3 ounces,
      (90 grams,
        145 yards)
  Crochet hook,
    size H (5.00 mm)

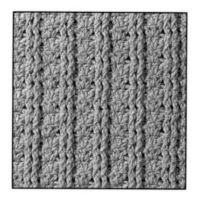

GAUGE: In pattern, 5 sts and 8 rows = 4"

Ch 46.

Row 1 (Right side): Dc in fourth ch from hook **(3 skipped chs count as first dc)**, ★ skip next 2 chs, 3 dc in next ch, skip next 2 chs, dc in next 2 chs; repeat from ★ across: 32 dc.

To work **Back Post double crochet (abbreviated BPdc)**, YO, insert hook from **back** to **front** around post of st indicated **(Fig. 1, page 1)**, YO and pull up a loop (3 loops on hook), (YO and draw through 2 loops on hook) twice. Skip st in front of BPdc.

Row 2: Ch 3 **(counts as first dc, now and throughout)**, turn; work BPdc around next dc, skip next dc, 3 dc in next dc, ★ skip next dc, work BPdc around each of next 2 dc, skip next dc, 3 dc in next dc; repeat from ★ across to last 3 dc, skip next dc, work BPdc around next dc, dc in last dc.

To work **Front Post double crochet (abbreviated FPdc)**, YO, insert hook from **front** to **back** around post of st indicated **(Fig. 1, page 1)**, YO and pull up a loop (3 loops on hook), (YO and draw through 2 loops on hook) twice. Skip dc behind FPdc.

Row 3: Ch 3, turn; work FPdc around next BPdc, skip next dc, 3 dc in next dc, ★ skip next dc, work FPdc around each of next 2 BPdc, skip next dc, 3 dc in next dc; repeat from ★ across to last 3 sts, skip next dc, work FPdc around next BPdc, dc in last dc.

Row 4: Ch 3, turn; work BPdc around next FPdc, skip next dc, 3 dc in next dc, ★ skip next dc, work BPdc around each of next 2 FPdc, skip next dc, 3 dc in next dc; repeat from ★ across to last 3 sts, skip next dc, work BPdc around next FPdc, dc in last dc.

Rows 5-18: Repeat Rows 3 and 4, 7 times; do **not** finish off.

EDGING

To work **Front Post single crochet (abbreviated FPsc)**, insert hook from **front** to **back** around post of st indicated **(Fig. 1, page 1)**, YO and pull up a loop (2 loops on hook), YO and draw through both loops on hook **(counts as one sc)**.

Rnd 1: Ch 1, turn; skip next BPdc, sc in sp before next dc and in next 3 dc, (work FPsc around next 2 FPdc, sc in next 3 dc) across to last 2 sts, sc in sp **before** next BPdc, ch 2; working in end of rows, [sc in sp between 2 sts at end of next row **(Fig. 11)**, ch 2] across; working in free loops **(Fig. 2b, page 1)** and in sps of beginning ch, 2 sc in first sp, sc in next ch and in next sp, work FPsc around next 2 dc, sc in next sp and in next ch, (sc in next sp, work FPsc around next 2 dc, sc in next sp and in next ch) 4 times, 2 sc in next sp, ch 2; working in end of rows, (sc in sp **between** 2 sts at end of next row, ch 2) across; join with slip st to first sc.

Fig. 11

Rnd 2: Ch 2 **(counts as first hdc, now and throughout)**, do **not** turn; hdc in each sc across, 3 hdc in last dc on Row 18; working behind Rnd 1 of Edging and in end of rows, hdc evenly across; 3 hdc in first ch of beginning ch, hdc in each sc across, 3 hdc in ch at base of last dc on Row 1; working behind Rnd 1 of Edging and in end of rows, hdc evenly across; 3 hdc in first dc on Row 18; join with slip st to first hdc.

Rnd 3: Ch 2, working in Back Loops Only, ★ hdc in each hdc across to center hdc of next corner 3-hdc group, 3 hdc in center hdc; repeat from ★ around to last hdc, hdc in last hdc; join with slip st to first hdc, finish off.

23. SHELLS & CLUSTERS

Finished Size: 10" x 9"

MATERIALS
100% Cotton
  Worsted Weight Yarn:
    2¼ ounces,
      (65 grams,
        110 yards)
Crochet hook,
  size F (3.50 mm)

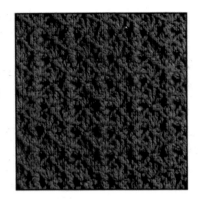

GAUGE: In pattern,
  (Shell, sc) 3 times = 4"; 8 rows = 3¼"

To work **Shell**, dc in st indicated, (ch 1, dc in same st) 3 times.

Ch 38.

Row 1 (Right side): Sc in second ch from hook, ★ skip next 2 chs, work Shell in next ch, skip next 2 chs, sc in next ch; repeat from ★ across: 6 Shells and 7 sc.

To work **beginning Cluster** (uses one st), YO, insert hook in same st, YO and pull up a loop, YO and draw through 2 loops on hook, YO and draw through one loop on hook, YO and draw through both loops on hook.

To work **Cluster** (uses one sc), ★ YO, insert hook in sc indicated, YO and pull up a loop, YO and draw through 2 loops on hook, YO and draw through one loop on hook; repeat from ★ once **more**, YO and draw through all 3 loops on hook.

Row 2: Ch 2, turn; work beginning Cluster, ★ ch 3, skip next ch-1 sp, sc in next ch-1 sp, ch 3, skip next 2 dc, work Cluster in next sc; repeat from ★ across: 6 Clusters and 12 ch-3 sps.

To work **Front Post single crochet** (abbreviated FPsc), insert hook from **front** to **back** around top of next Cluster (*Fig. 1, page 1*), YO and pull up a loop (2 loops on hook) YO and draw through both loops on hook (counts as one sc).

Row 3: Ch 1, turn; sc in first Cluster, work Shell in next sc, ★ work FPsc, work Shell in next sc; repeat from ★ across to last 2 dc, skip next dc, sc in last dc: 6 Shells and 7 sc.

Rows 4-17: Repeat Rows 2 and 3, 7 times.

Row 18: Ch 1, turn; sc in first sc, ★ ch 2, skip next ch-1 sp, sc in next ch-1 sp, ch 2, skip next 2 dc, sc in next sc; repeat from ★ across; do **not** finish off.

EDGING
Rnd 1: Ch 3 (**counts as first dc, now and throughout**), turn; 2 dc in each of next 2 ch-2 sps, ★ dc in next sc, 2 dc in each of next 2 ch-2 sps; repeat from ★ across to last sc, (dc, ch 3, dc) in last sc; work 29 dc evenly spaced across end of rows; working in free loops (*Fig. 2b, page 1*) and in sps across beginning ch, (dc, ch 3, dc) in first ch, 2 dc in each of next 2 sps, (dc in next ch, 2 dc in each of next 2 sps) 5 times, (dc, ch 3, dc) in next ch; work 29 dc evenly spaced across end of rows; dc in same st as first dc, ch 3; join with slip st to first dc: 124 dc.

To work **Front Post double crochet** (abbreviated FPdc), YO, insert hook from **front** to **back** around post of next dc (*Fig. 1, page 1*), YO and pull up a loop (3 loops on hook), (YO and draw through 2 loops on hook) twice.

Rnd 2: Ch 3, do **not** turn; (work FPdc, dc in next dc) across to next corner ch-3 sp, (dc, ch 3, dc) in corner ch-3 sp, ★ dc in next dc, (work FPdc, dc in next dc) across to next corner ch-3 sp, (dc, ch 3, dc) in corner ch-3 sp; repeat from ★ 2 times **more**; join with slip st to first dc, finish off.